THE PORTAGE POETRY SERIES

SERIES TITLES

Dear Lo
Brady Bove

Sadness of the Apex Predator
Dion O'Reilly

Do Not Feed the Animal
Hikari Miya

The Watching Sky
Judy Brackett Crowe

Let It Be Told in a Single Breath
Russell Thorburn

The Blue Divide
Linda Nemec Foster

Lake, River, Mountain
Mark B. Hamilton

Talking Diamonds
Linda Nemec Foster

Poetic People Power
Tara Bracco (ed.)

The Green Vault Heist
David Salner

There is a Corner of Someplace Else
Camden Michael Jones

Everything Waits
Jonathan Graham

We Are Reckless
Christy Prahl

Always a Body
Molly Fuller

Bowed As If Laden With Snow
Megan Wildhood

Silent Letter
Gail Hanlon

New Wilderness
Jenifer DeBellis

Fulgurite
Catherine Kyle

The Body Is Burden and Delight
Sharon White

Bone Country
Linda Nemec Foster

Not Just the Fire
R.B. Simon

Monarch
Heather Bourbeau

The Walk to Cefalù
Lynne Viti

The Found Object Imagines a Life: New and Selected Poems
Mary Catherine Harper

Naming the Ghost
Emily Hockaday

Mourning
Dokubo Melford Goodhead

Messengers of the Gods: New and Selected Poems
Kathryn Gahl

After the 8-Ball
Colleen Alles

Careful Cartography
Devon Bohm

Broken On the Wheel
Barbara Costas-Biggs

Sparks and Disperses
Cathleen Cohen

Holding My Selves Together: New and Selected Poems
Margaret Rozga

Lost and Found Departments
Heather Dubrow

Marginal Notes
Alfonso Brezmes

The Almost-Children
Cassondra Windwalker

Meditations of a Beast
Kristine Ong Muslim

Pandora's Prairie

Katherine Hoerth's *Pandora's Prairie* documents the personal angst-filled days of barrenness so many in this world are fighting through. In every sunrise and daily interaction, she finds herself continually battling the dark of depression the Fates put upon us. From her earliest time as a child "… Outside, (my father) tended to/an Eden that I couldn't wait to leave.", Hoerth finds herself "…A victim of the times" in her struggle to create a life out of the nothingness she feels trapped in, once even seeming to shout forth: "This ice cream is a metaphor for rage." There is emptiness. There is a longing for something beyond our power to know; the collective heartbrokenness of the human experience.

—KARLA K. MORTON
2010 Texas State Poet Laureate
author of *Turbulence & Fluids*

In reading these Midwestern pastoral poems, I kept thinking of how they were like Robert Frost using the New England landscape's flora and fauna to understand the most profound human concerns and emotions of everyday life. And unlike the Pandora of myth, Hoerth opens herself up in a poignant, deeply personal, honest, and insightful way, reflecting on the delicate balance between nature's simplicity and human life's complexities. This poetry is timeless and rich, and like in her poem, "Headlights," the reader will find, after the many moments artfully examining daily life's dilemmas, that *the streets ahead are bathed in gold.*

—DAVID M. PARSONS
2011 Texas State Poet Laureate
author of *Austin Relativity: Coming of Age in the '60s*

Pandora's Prairie

poems

Katherine Hoerth

CORNERSTONE PRESS
UNIVERSITY OF WISCONSIN-STEVENS POINT

Cornerstone Press, Stevens Point, Wisconsin 54481
Copyright © 2025 Katherine Hoerth
www.uwsp.edu/cornerstone

Printed in the United States of America.

Library of Congress Control Number: 2025941888
ISBN: 978-1-968148-01-0

Cornerstone Press titles are produced in courses and internships offered by the
Department of English at the University of Wisconsin–Stevens Point.

DIRECTOR & PUBLISHER
Dr. Ross K. Tangedal

EXECUTIVE EDITORS
Jeff Snowbarger, Freesia McKee

EDITORIAL DIRECTOR
Brett Hill

SENIOR EDITORS
Paige Biever, Eva Nielsen, Reilly Crous

PRESS STAFF
Karlie Harpold, Josh Paulson, Aja Woolley, Ryleigh Miller, Mydasia Zipperer, Abby
Paulsen, Sophie McPherson, Sam Bjork, Madison Schultz, Autumn Vine, Allison
Lange

For Bruno and August

CONTENTS

I. ASUNDER

II. PRAIRIE MADNESS

III. BROKEN INTO BLOSSOM

I.

ASUNDER

At Lewis and Clark Landing

Another perfect April afternoon
along the river: spring is in full bloom,
the marigolds show off their amber hues
in flowerboxes, patches of fresh-laid sod
shimmer with an embarrassment of green.
Young catalpas planted in a row
along the loamy shoreline settle in—ideal
for their shallow roots and fragrant flowers.

A toddler races to the brand-new sandbox
with a shovel in her hand. She'll dig,
perhaps to China, fill her pail with earth.
A swing set moans as someone breaks it in.
The jungle gym, with wet paint, sits untouched.

The Missouri River lazes on
through the season as it has for eons,
before it had this name, before it carved
this landing place of history and lead.
Beneath the thin veneer of peace, what lies?
A foot of clay, a superfund, the bones
of the past. We've covered up such darkness here.
We pray our children never dig too deep.

Pandora in 2020

Years have passed. She holds her empty box
and the weight of chaos on her chest.
She recalls the split—how all the clocks
seemed to stop at once, how all the rest
is myth: the lid slipped off and everything
flew out of darkness like a ragged cough
into the sky's voracious maw to bring
the law of entropy, to set it off

upon our messy world. Today, she knows
countless others share her burden, heavy
in the lungs, the heart, the pit. The nose
contains a thousand droplets, each one ready
to be sent into the world, to drift,
to be opened like an unexpected gift.

Tornado Watch

I love it when the sky glows green, the color
of fecundity. And yes, it means disaster
might be over the horizon, swirling
up in the abyss of this, our plains.
I listen to the pattering of raindrops
on the roof. I smell the scent of life
carried on the violent gusts of wind.
Lightning slices through the skin of sky
and the moans of thunder shake the house.
As cumulonimbus clouds begin to twist
and slip into the sodden earth below,
I can't help but fix my eyes ahead
on what's to come for all of us who live
our days in a monotony of seasons.
I feel it in my flesh: the kick of change
that soon will sweetly tear our lives asunder.

Summers of Lightning Bugs

Once, I loved you like a firefly—
remember how they used to make the fields

effulgent like the midnight sky once was?
When this was orange fields and the heart

grew wild like the meadow? Do you remember
how each year those lightning bugs return

like spring, cicada songs, and wild pigeons?
How their lightshow made of everything

that moves our bodies lit this backyard up?
And one by one, some darkness snuffed the fire—

little mistakes like leaving porchlights on,
the city's growing glow, the giant flares,

those blazing elephants we can't ignore
in the onyx skies that are our lives.

Now, it's night again. It's summer, too.
Now I'm sipping bourbon on the porch

gazing into fields of emptiness,
wondering what mountains I must move

to make those lightning bugs return to us.

The Golden Hour, Chalco Hills

You walk the trails of western Omaha,
your camera hanging from your neck. It's cold
this afternoon, but still you're here to watch
the tundra geese come home to roost at dusk.

You tuck your hands inside your jacket pockets.
Soon, the golden hour will melt to gloam.
You stop and gaze into a patch of tallgrass
swaying in a gust of arctic air.

You notice how the purple florets catch
amber rays within their tiny hairs,
shimmering with light for but an instant.
Your camera snaps. You freeze the frame in time,

like a sneak of smile, before night
returns and brings the wind, before your fingers
turn to ice, before the sun, like joy,
descends with haste into the cold horizon.

Trying to Conceive in 2020

The ovulation test displays a smile
this morning. A kaleidoscope of viceroys
take flight within your gut. You grin, a fool
giddy for tonight, the possibility
of what's to come. You stare down at the test
as it sits atop the bathroom counter.
The world outside the door begins to melt
away like winter's snow, and all you see
is eternal spring within your mind:
snapdragons popping back to life again
in shades of baby pink, the rabbit kits
rustling the tallgrass of the prairie,
a clutch of robin eggs, cerulean
and tucked inside a nest within a willow.

But summer's getting longer every year.
A derecho strips the willow of her branches
and the nest comes tumbling to the concrete.
A bulldozer tears up the rabbits' burrow
on the quest to make this prairie thrive
into suburbia with perfect houses,
emerald lawns, and lovely picket fences—
the ideal neighborhood for families
like yours may be. Your gut becomes a pit.
You hold back this feeling like a cough
and fixate on that smile, that smile, that smile.

The Recipe for Fudge

Because I have a sweet tooth just like hers,
my mother says she'll teach me how to make
grandma's secret fudge. Let it be known:
I love the taste, the memories it brings,
the scent of chocolate wafting through the kitchen,

the grit of sugar sticking to my teeth.
I crave, I long for one more taste of her—
the way she knew to love, a wooden spoon,
no need for a thermometer, she read
the sheen of chocolate like an open palm

and knew exactly when to beat the batter
and when to let it cool. Her fudge was love
in bitesize squares. I always left her house
with armfuls of her fudge, an aching belly
and a face stained umber. Love like this

can rot the teeth, can spoil the appetite,
can poison blood, a river full of sugar
flowing through the tired pancreas.
So. when my mother tells me that she'll teach
me how to make this fudge, I hesitate.

I think of grandma, knee-deep in her sickness,
making batches for the ones she loves
and sneaking little nibbles for herself.
She loved until it hurt, and when she died,
my mother soon became the queen of fudge,

slinging batches in her kitchen, keeping
memories of grandma on the tongue,

or in the belly, filling up the flesh of her,
of her, of me. Sugar of her sugar,
blood of blood, fresh fudge atop the table

cooling in afternoon's long laze,
my mother grins with grains of sugar grit
between her teeth. I have no choice, I'll learn
to love like this, to love with sweetness hard
until it hurts, until it kills—embrace
of cocoa, kiss of candy, nourishment
of full-fat milk, a couple pats of butter,
the plundered center of vanilla beans,
heaps of joy. The hardest part is waiting
for the fudge to cool. My mother watches

with the glinted simper of her mother,
of me, our blood a muddy river flooded
with sugar, saccharine, and love that flows
through the veins, into the heart, the glucose
inundating, rising, falling, ebbing.

I take a piece of candy from the dish,
remember grandma as it starts to melt
atop my tongue. I take the recipe
into myself, the recipe for love
all the women in my family know by heart.

Sunday Mornings

My father didn't know a day of rest.
Even Sundays, he would get up early,
dress in shorts and sandals to head out
to the grocery store before the morning rush.
He'd drive into the shimmering dawn, return
home with heavy sacks of milk and honey—
I never thought to praise him. But I'd wake
to the lawn mower's hymn and curse the noise
that roused me out of bed, and in my slippers,
I would stumble to the kitchen, always find
an apple fritter waiting just for me.
This was our Sunday ritual of sweets
and sacrifice. Outside, he tended to
an Eden that I couldn't wait to leave.

Last Trick-or-Treat

Girl, can you see the horizon
assembling into something more
than simple sunset? Suburbia darkens
as the streetlights click on.
A black cat slinks out from the hedges,
the ones your neighbor keeps neat and trimmed.
Tonight, these perfect yards
wear garlands of graveyards,
set out jack-o-lanterns
that grin and beckon you
to the doorstep to taste
the sweetness of childhood
one last time. The fanged moon rises,

drapes your bony shoulders in shimmer.
For now, your breath smells of Starburst
and your tongue is stained with Skittles.
This is how you learn to laugh at fear:
following porchlights like a moth
and opening your plastic pumpkin
to receive the final harvest of childhood.

But once the sun has fully disappeared,
and once the streetlights all click on,
and once that sugar high has faded into memory,
you'll find out who the real monsters are.

Prairie Verbena

February 2021

No one thought a freeze would come this late—
least of all, verbena blossoms, young
and too naïve to know that February
is a liar with a silver tongue.

A couple balmy afternoons, the warm
tongue of sunshine, dulcet trill of purple martins
blasting like a love song through a bedroom
window, invited every bloom to come
and dance. The soft breeze whispered promises
of a gentle spring, an everlasting summer
filled with warm nights and the pattering
of raindrops—all the things a sweet verbena
needs to thrive. And so, the wildflower
peeked her head up from the earth and opened
the bud, unfurled those petals to the sky

that turned to slate, encased her face in ice,
and smothered her in snow. Verbena blossom,
now the color of a nasty bruise,
limp and shorn, will never hold her head
so high again. A victim of the times

that bloomed too fast, this prairie wildflower—
like a girl, yes always, like a girl.

Ode to the Dudes Who Wear Shorts in Winter

I admire you for your defiance
of the season's change. I know you're cold—
shoveling mounds of snow and salting sidewalks,
your cheeks the color of a McIntosh,
your skin awash in gooseflesh, ice
crusting on your eyelashes like sleep.

I must admit, you look ridiculous
as most folks bundle up in coats and boots
and common sense. Oh naked-legged warrior,
you prefer the heat your muscles make.
You wear your masculinity in place
of a cozy scarf, and may it keep
you warm this late November afternoon.

I salute you, dude outside in shorts,
as I sip a cup of apple cider.
You believe in summer, all it is:
the warmth, its bright fecundity,
its bliss. You live for this, reminding me
of what we leave behind each year
and what's ahead of us if we hang on
through these dreary months of grey and cold.

You fight the good fight, standing in the way
of frost and everything it represents:
the slowing down, the barrenness, the ending
of another year that passes us.

I know your teeth are chattering in silence.
I know your bones are aching just like mine.
I know your hair is turning white as snow.

Is it denial, faith, or something else
that fills you with the warmth no pants can give?
Oh dude in shorts, and all your brethren,
keep raging on against the dying season.

Ode to Mayonnaise

You are my shame—a glob of whiteness slathered
between the brioche and arugula,
a slick of fat that glides across my teeth,
the alabaster jiggle of my thighs.

Mayo, flavor of my childhood
in a small Wisconsin town where everyone
had skin the color of your glossy dollop,
I must confess you are a part of me,
though I pretend to savor other flavors
like Dijon, siracha, or picante.
Deep down, you are the condiment I crave
for the comfort of your mouthfeel on my tongue.

I can't deny myself the creaminess,
the spoiled taste of privilege I eat
slipped secretly between two hunks of bread.

Mayonnaise—ambrosia in a tub,
heaping scoops of white potato salad,
that little extra something in the dip
that makes it taste like it's some miracle
of my own creation, I need you,
but I know you're made of nothing good
for the body, spirit, or the soul.

Mayonnaise, you are my secret weapon.
You are my ignorance. You are my whiteness.

You are the shiny cloak I wear, the yolk
that hinges me to history, the sins
of my ancestors, the ones who gave
me an appetite for mayonnaise.

Another Autumn Day Downtown

Downtown bustles like a factory
of humanity. The intersection
hums with troubled order—green, then yellow,
then sanguine. Suddenly, a car plows through

as horns blare and tires scream. The car
thrusts to the curb, the grass. A building stops
it in its path. A clash of metal, then
an eerie quiet hangs above the street.

No one emerges from the car. The door
is sealed shut. Inside, the driver slumps
over the steering wheel, an empty vessel.
The city pulses on. No sign of stopping.

The traffic light turns green and red again,
and office workers bustle past the scene,
coffee thermoses in hand as steam
arises with the scent of work. It's autumn—

leaves have fallen everywhere in silence.
Soon, the sirens rise above the heartbeat
of this city as a firetruck parts
the humdrum sea with lights the hue of blood.

Two men pop out in unison, begin
their choreography of miracles:
one breaks the window of the car and pops
the lock. The other wheels out a stretcher.

They pull the driver out. Her eyes roll back
into her skull, her body but a prop,

a thing to carry off into the darkness
of the truck. They ferry off their cargo

and disappear into the whirring distance.
The landscape fills the empty space with wind,
blowing the memory like fallen leaves.
Meanwhile, I, a weary witness, weep.

Portrait of the Goddess at the Village Inn

Council Bluffs, Iowa

So many people asking for so much,
she lets out an exasperated sigh
as she shuffles back into the kitchen
to pick up another round of plates
to feed the hungry mouths that fill this place.

Each plate contains a world—a plain of pancakes,
nacho mountains, bowls of chicken soup
like oceans that she ferries on her arms,
dropping nothing to the dingy carpet
beneath her tired feet. You ask for something.
She listens, brings it to you in her time—
a fork, a napkin, or Tabasco sauce.

Some thank her; others don't and think that blessings
fall upon them from the sky and not
her calloused hands. Her eyes are deep and dark,
her makeup's smudged, her apron wears the stains
of everybody in this world. No matter,

she still rules this diner like a kingdom,
knows the cost of everybody's sins
and tabulates them on her little notebook,
makes sure everybody pays before
they leave into the cold and dreary world
beyond these walls. The lunch rush never ends—

you watch her from your corner booth and sip
coffee from a cup that always brims
by some miracle of her creation.
Before you settle up your bill, she slips

a something on the table with a wink
and tells you, *Child, it's on the house*, but no,
you don't deserve such kindness. After all,
you're just another hungry mouth to feed,
and yet, it's there before you like a boon—
a slice of apple pie as sweet as Eden.

Brown December

The snow is late to come in Omaha—
it's December and the landscape still
looks flat and barren, mile after mile
of exhausted fields and faded tallgrass.

A gray sky hangs above. There should be snow.
It's that time of the month, but nothing falls.
There should be icicles alight like eyes
in wonderment. This vista should be curved
with snowdrifts, round like bellies. Clouds should sag
heavy with snow, the forecasters expecting,

school children praying for it. You can't help
but wonder if the earth is finished giving
snowflakes—if those dawns of miracles
when you awake, look out your window, see
your whole world suddenly transformed, now pure
and glimmering with promise of the sound
of children's laughter as they sled, build snowmen,
make boot prints in the blanketing of snow,

are over. Why bring snowflakes to this world
of flare stacks and despair? Of melting, warming
and exhaust? You've squandered snow days, cursing
those pesky stains of snowmelt on the floor,
the ache of cold, its kiss on your flush cheeks.

Now you're gazing at the graying sky,
yearning for a blizzard, one last chance
to spread your legs and arms to make an angel
in your image, to feel that flurry deep
within your flesh before your season ends.

My Grandma Creates the Earth

In science class, I learned the earth was made
from dust and gas leftover from the sun's
miraculous creation, that it scraped
together pieces of itself and formed
a feast of sea and land, of sky and life.

But none of this made any sense to me—
I'd studied the geography of worry
on the pages of my mother's face,
the tilted axis of her head, a bend
of frown, a riverbed around her eyes,
the canyons of her forehead as she'd find
once again more month than dollars tucked
inside the somber cavern of her purse.

I'd come to understand that folks like us
made do with what they had inside their pantries—
scraping the empty peanut butter jar,
mouthfuls of stale bread, saltines with ketchup.
But how could something beautiful be born
of scraps, of what another threw away?

One autumn dusk, my grandma came to visit
on the last day of September, filled
the kitchen with her presence and the bustling
sounds of cooking—whisk on pan, a hiss
and cackle sound of oil, a bang of pots.
She emptied out the sack of flour, cracked
expired eggs into a bowl. She poured
a swig of sour milk and toasted bread butts,
declared the miracle of Sunday supper,
created from the nothing of the cupboard.

Pancakes rolled, a gold expanse of prairie,
a hill of butter, rivering with syrup,
fluffy clouds of eggs, plateau of toast
smeared with sanguine jelly. Grandma gazed
at my hungry eyes, my mother's smile
as she came home from work to find this feast.
Grandma sat down at the table, sighed,
said grace, and knew that it was good.

Manifest Destiny

God anointed you the caretaker
of this prairie. Mold it in your image
acre after acre after acre.

First, you beat the wildness out of her—
the gamma grass, the brambles, and the brimming
patches of leadplant. You're the caretaker

with a plow, an ox, a boot print. Nature
won't easily surrender. She's like Lilith—
acre after acre after acre

of struggle—stubborn sod, a tiny crater
then a million of them dug by timid
marmots, tickseed. You're the caretaker

and after endless hours of grueling labor,
you will make wild wasteland grimace
in rows of fertile rows that cover acre

after acre. You're the vindicator
of this land, won't stop until you're finished,
and acre after acre after acre
bows, with gold, to you, the great caretaker.

For My Brother

My little brother was afraid of darkness—
a plug-in nightlight kept his fear at bay.

My little brother was a white-skinned boy
who blazed and blistered in the Midwest sun,
who had a sweet tooth, chased the ice cream truck,
who slugged a couple cans of Mountain Dew
each day, a game controller in his hands.

My brother with his always stinky socks,
my brother with his cotton-colored hair,
my brother with a face that's rubescent—

I'm grateful that he had a chance to grow
out of his T-rex sandals and exchange
them for a leather pair of Harley boots
and the angry scowl on his face.

Tonight, I'm sitting by a lambent campfire
wondering where he is in this great world.
I think of him each time a flare stack blooms,
or I strike a match, or see a tiki torch
catching fire in Charlottesville, my brother.

Tonight, I mourn the man that he became
in the dark nights of his fear, the men
at his side—each one was once a boy
like him with nightlights glowing in their bedrooms.
Tonight, I mourn the hate that blisters skin,
the spit that flies from mouths, the firepit
within the burning belly of their being.

My brother—white and fragile like a lamb,
trembling in his racecar bed, he asks
me to read him one more bedtime story
before I flick the switch and darkness fills
his room, his sky-blue eyes, his raging heart.
I wipe my brother's tears and kiss his forehead.

Then he's gone, my little brother, gone,
chasing fires like nightlights in the sky.

The Smell of Spring

I breathe in the scents of early spring:
the honeyed morning breath of yarrow blossoms,
the smell of sunrays slicing through the still
air like a sharpened knife straight through a lemon,

the weeping of mowed grass, the aftermath
a rainstorm leaves with standing puddles, sodden
branches, and so many fallen leaves,
the melting of another season—winter,

and everything that dredges up again
with a waft of rot of anyone
who didn't make it through the bitter months,
like a brown bat fallen from the nest

or a groundhog frozen in its burrow,
or the grief that I encased in ice.
The world around this body starts to bloom,
perfumes me with its complicated scent.

Pandora's Box of Seeds

Who opened up Pandora's box of seeds?
Before, these grasses grew as high as hips—
the purpletop, the junegrass, and the dropseed.
Indiangrass once filled this swathe of land.
You remember how in late September
their plumes would paint the vista with the colors
of dawn and dusk for farther than the eye
can see, and how they nourished everything
that makes this ecosystem flourish—drowned
in a sea of roots: of quackgrass, brome,
Caucasian bluestem scattering across
the meadow like a thousand grains of salt
spilled on the kitchen floor, impossible
to pick them up again with just your fingers.

You wonder how it happened all so fast—
how easily Pandora slipped the lid
from the box and let this nightmare loose,
how this landscape metamorphosized
from paradise to farmland then to suburbs.
You shake your head. You know what's coming next.

You kneel in your garden, planting hope
in pockets full of prairie. Not enough.
You know you're just another seedling growing
in another row of flaxen grains.
You dig your roots into this fertile loam.

II.

PRAIRIE MADNESS

Prairie Madness

West Omaha, 2020

The scent of weeping pine trees fills the air.
Instead of crow caws, drill songs ride the wind.
An avenue named Rosewood copperheads
through a neighborhood, suburbia.

The houses grow like stalks in rows, each one
planted carefully, a verdant promise
of tomorrow, reaching towards the blue
Nebraska sky, the openness of it.

How full of gold it feels today: the morning
sunshine bathing all the roofs in butter,
the gold of rings on every finger here,
its history of grain and humble farmers

with their forlorn wives out on the plains,
the harvest and the emptiness that follows.
I'm standing in the middle of it all,
staring out my window at the neighbor

jogging past, her hair like mine, the hue
of cornsilk, wheat, a field of grain, our bodies—
all of us in rows of loneliness
driven to madness by the prairie wind.

Eve, Quarantined

Is this how she felt millennia
ago while sheltering in Eden's refuge?

Like her, I want for nothing in this place.
My cupboard's filled with bags of rice and beans.
My freezer's stocked with chicken, beef, and pork.
The bedroom blooms with pleasure like a garden.

The only thing that's missing is the sun—
red like apples, cherries, pomegranates
setting against the backdrop of a city
that's now a ghost town. Standing in her garden,

naked, did she gaze beyond the walls
of her home, like I do every dusk,
looking out the window, smudging it
with her palms, and weep for what she misses?

This fragile flesh, these fragile bones, be damned.
Mortality and paradise be damned.

Is this the ache she felt within her heart
to get back to the toil of the living?

December Derecho

You're learning to accept the unexpected—
not expect, accept. The snow's all melted

in December and the grass springs greenly
from the ground as though it's April. Sweetly,

robins serenade the warming morning
from their empty nests as storms are forming

to the west. This shouldn't be: a wall
of clouds erecting in the sky, a whorl

of prairie dust and fallen leaves, a siren
quickening your breath, the whole horizon

suddenly uncertain as a redux
spring blows in and sweeps away the harvest's husks.

What else to do but hurry to the basement
and watch in both parts horror and amazement

as the sky turns green as spring and you
feel the season running fingers through

your tousled hair and billowing your skirt—
awakening again your windswept heart.

The News

Somehow, the roly-polies missed the news—
they keep on moving earth beneath our feet.
I want to tell them that the world is ending,
wake them from their joy. I want to ask
them why they keep on working,
toiling, turning the debris of winter
into spring if spring may never bloom.
I want to whisper in their little ears
that the world today's a dangerous place,
to go home to their dens, to ride this season
of death out underneath a mask of earth.

The grackles seem oblivious as well
clustering on powerlines together
as sunlight seeps into the morning sky
and brings them back to life. The doves are mourning
like they always do. The mockingbirds,
who have so much to grieve, rebuild a nest
that tumbled to ground in last night's storm.
I want to ask them why they even bother.

The lovegrass keeps on swaying, growing, taking
over my unkept lawn. It clenches dirt
in its fists of roots and spreads and spreads
like a yawn or sneeze or cough. The dew
this morning doesn't know, or if it does
it still sparkles, pearls on blades of grass.

I want to tell the old mesquite tree
before she bursts in yellow blooms again.
And I want to tell the beetles, the mosquitos,
the flies, the mushrooms at my feet, the stones,

though maybe they've seen worse than this before
in their timeless lives. And when they learn,
as I have, that our world is ending soon,
the roly-polies keep on moving earth—
as they always have for centuries,
making the world go round and round and round
as they bring it back to life again.

Wild Raspberries

There's nothing quite like stumbling upon
a bramble hidden in the forest's shade
with a sudden burst of burgundy
or the mauve of perfect ripening

weighing down a branch or maybe two.
You pluck the berries. They come willingly
into your palm and leave a sticky stain
on your fingertips that, hours later,

you'll lick for an aftertaste of this
sweet and tangy afternoon of nothing
to do but stroll. How rare, these fleeting moments,
how rare, this taste of wilderness, the scent

of leaves unfurling at your touch, the feeling
that this trail will wind forever. Soon,
this lazy Sunday afternoon will end.
Soon, you'll head back into the city where

raspberries languish in your fridge, a carton
of them from a farm out west. They're drenched
in pesticides. They have an aftertaste
of consumerism—dry with just a hint

of joy, enough to keep your stomach wanting
raspberry-ness. The real thing, these brambles
grow wild between suburbia and city
as the farmland stretches endlessly,

acres of it, so much gold and green,
the same for miles and miles, and days and days,
through life, extending into the horizon
then the prairie sky, with bits of sweet

serendipity like this to break
up the monotony. You'll crave this taste
after you leave this trail, this nook of forest.
After you return to life, this week

you'll dream of wilderness, a day not plowed
into the neat and perfect rows of corn,
like the earth, the hours of your day
gone feral. Have you felt like this before?

You run your tongue across the crimson stain
on your teeth, your lips, your heart, that marks
you as a beast who's tasted something more
than golden grain and verdant emptiness.

My Father, Howling

By day, my father was a teacher—straight-laced,
carrying a briefcase and smile
everywhere he'd go. But once it's dark,
after he brings me milk and cookies, reads
a bedtime story, kisses me
on the forehead, he would disappear
out to the back porch, and sit beneath
the moon, a banjo in his arms, and croon.

Cradling his banjo like a daughter,
he'd sing a lullaby to someone else—
one filled with longing and his memories
of bluegrass days, of picking strings and apples,
of whiskey breath and his own father's hands—
calloused, rough, and nothing like his own.

He'd sing of mountain dew, of running through
a place called cripple creek. He'd beg the sky
to bury him beneath a willow tree
as the perfectly trimmed cypresses
that lined our quiet neighborhood were swaying
to the tapping of his tired, naked feet.

He'd finish up the set with one last song:
Amazing Grace. He'd belt it out to God,
whom he'd lost his faith in years ago,
but felt the spirit of the night out here
in the Eden of suburbia,
a place that maybe never felt like home.

House, Left Unfinished

One day, the workers all packed up and left
the house's bones exposed, the driveway halfway
paved, garage without a door, a gaping
wound. I pass it on my way to work
each day and wonder why things shrivel up
while others bloom. I wonder who conceived
this castle in the sky that fell apart.

I wonder if the wife dreamed of its face
smiling at her with its pearly pickets,
if the husband bought a riding mower,
ready to tend unruly wilderness,
nurture it into a perfect lawn
he could brag about to everyone.

But there it sits, alone, becoming dust,
returning to the earth like all things do
eventually, this house before its time,
before it had the chance to feel bare feet
against its tiles, to echo laughter, glow
with love at midnight from a bedroom window
as chuck-wills-widows trill their lullabies.

Dear Sarah

Dear Sarah, if only I too could laugh
in the face of this, another cold morning,
frost encrusting prairie grass, snuffing out
hope like those first shades of green
after so many months of nothing.

Sarah, I'm so tired of wintercrearig,
the color of joy perpetually sapped
from this season that should be spring.

Sarah, how many times did your flesh
flutter with hope? How many months
were you disappointed when nothing grew
in the flowerbed of your body,
even as the ice in the rivers within you
melted to slush, and you saw it, a cardinal

set against the white snow. Sarah, this afternoon,
after another visit to the OBGYN,
we went to the park to walk, to feel spring
finally coaxing the grass to grow green again,

to try again. Sarah, you can't stop hope
from welling in your heart, can you?

Sarah, God never stops the rosebuds
from filling this prairie with red.

Cherry Strudel

This is how I deal with disappointment:
Baking strudel. It's something one must practice

to get good at. My first time was a mess
of sticky cherries, gummy dough, and scalded sugar

on the pan that took weeks of scrubbing to be rid of.
Since then, I've learned to work with dough

that's difficult: knead it carefully with patience
until it finally obeys the fingertips' commands,

to let it breathe a moment in between such kneading,
to chop the cherries small to quell the sour tang—

a mouth can only take so much, to sieve the sugar
so it doesn't clot, a little sweetness goes a long way,

and oh, I've learned to not be shy with butter.
It smooths over everything with gold.

The seams are hardest to get right. You can't
stuff a strudel too full of fruit or else,

the inevitable. High heat is good for crispy edges,
yes, but too hot and it explodes. I knead. I mix. I chop.

I wrap. I seal. I slice a couple holes in the top
to let this pastry breathe. I breathe, then pop it in the oven,

slam shut the door, and for a moment,
forget this whole ordeal. Soon, the house

will smell of sweetness. Soon, I'll pat my back,
wonder how I've gotten so good

at dealing with tough dough,
with sour cherries, and with loss.

But even sometimes, now, like today,
the strudel ruptures, a pool of crimson

cherry juice seeps out from the seam,
the seam I've carefully clasped shut

to no avail. It couldn't handle this today—
the heat of the oven, the failings of my flesh,

the moon. And at the sight of it, I, too,
in my floured apron, in my messy kitchen,

burst.

The Horsefly in the New House

The sound of buzzing fills the empty house.
It echoes on the walls, the tiles, the ceiling,
the only thing that occupies this space—
a horsefly bangs its body on a window.

We enter in, new occupants of this
land of bleach and sun, imagining
our life unfolding here, and there it is:
a big black bug, a dusty kitchen window,
and the heart. I wonder just how long
it's been here in this emptiness, alone,
hurling itself against a sheet of glass
that won't give way no matter what it does,
dreaming perhaps of that blue sky it sees
but doesn't taste or smell except in longing
for the dulcet fragrance of a mare's
worry, the eager aster's morning breath.

I hear its buzzing as our coming stirs
it once again to try again. She hurls
herself against the window, bounces to the sill,
then revs her wings. It's futile but she doesn't
know that yet or if she does, she can't
give up, not now. It isn't in her guts.

I feel that buzzing in my heart as well—
how it feels to bang your battered body
against a thing that just won't give, no matter
what you do, a sheet of glass, a window
to a world that you can see but never
feel within your flesh, the open sky
egging you on and calling out your name.

The fly rests for a moment as my husband
opens the window, and in wafts the smell
of the wild, of fecundity
at these final months of spring. The fly
reawakens, flings herself against the screen
again, again, again, again, again.

I shoo 'her off. My husband looks at me
with an ounce of mercy in his gaze
just enough to feed a horsefly hope.
He removes the screen methodically, and then,
the fly, one final time, collects her scraps
of strength and flings herself into the wind.

I watch the sky devour her. The buzzing
fades to wind, and in that single moment,
my body longs to be a horsefly, too.

A Visit from Joy

He sojourns to my window dressed in emerald
plumage every year around this time.
A fleeting moment of elation hovers
at the glass, its long and narrow beak
ideal for sousing out a bit of sweetness.
Maybe this time he'll stay awhile, I think.

How did he end up here—this concrete jungle
of my heart? This is no place for him—
winged joy in search of dulcet nourishment.
He's miles away from where he ought to be—
the flyway, forest, prairie in full bloom
where nothing stops a smile from unfurling
at the sight of so much purple phlox.

But still, he perches on a branch and stares
through my window, at my eyes, expecting
me to offer him a reason he might linger.
A hanging pot of salvias, perhaps?
A plastic feeder filled with sugared water?
At least a little shade where he can rest?

This empty yard is not your breeding ground.
I am no paradise nor an oasis—
just a barren landscape to be crossed.

Joy understands. He needs a fertile heart
in which to build his nest. Mine isn't right.
He buzzes off into the fragrant distance
and disappears into a world of blue.

White Tail Doe

My headlights scintillate the crust of frost
blanketing this meadow. The clouds above
snuff out all moon or starlight. Suddenly,
a flash of white breaks through the beam: the tail

of a doe. It's only me and her.
Something makes me stop my car, roll down
my window and outstretch my hand. She freezes.
Her doe-eyes widen into spheres of dusk.

What have they seen that fills them with such fear?
My headlights shine like sunbeams through the frost,
and for this moment, everything's alight—
inviting magic or a miracle.

Maybe for both of us this time is different.
The doe locks eyes with me as if to test
her faith against her instinct and her past.
Perhaps a car, like hope, can shatter more

than bones. She turns towards darkness once again,
a home that's always held her in its arms,
where light and warmth can't touch her anymore—
and with a sudden rustling, she's gone

into a place my heart knows all too well.

Nebraska Antipastoral

A cottontail awakens in the thicket
of your mind. Your cheeks are full of bluestem,
dropseed, lovegrass, purpletop, and foxtail.
A feral story thumping in these haunches,
twitching in these ears, and widening

these raven eyes. You want to just stand still
but you find your body thrusted forth with hunger
and fear in equal measure. Your incisors
carve no words morning. Understand?
You sink into the thickets full of rabbitbrush,

preyed upon or not. You know the clover
from the flavor of a coneflower,
the difference in the cries of crows and hawks,
the blinding beauty of an open field.
Don't you see? You're tuft and scurry, shedding

last season's ego like a winter coat.
You are all eyes and dart and heart and cower,
the urge to make the most of spring's forgiveness.
You have fallen from the fantasy
of progress: perfect rows of golden corn,

a lawn of manicured St. Augustine,
white picket fences, clotheslines with fresh sheets,
into your own forgotten reverie.
How could you know what hibernated in
the snug and secret burrow of the psyche?

Dear Noah,

I bet you never looked at rain the same,
did you, after the flood? When you were young,
did you love the rain like so many do?

The romance of a distant thunder rolling in,
the smell of the earth's must, its longing for it,
the way it urges you to spend the afternoon in bed?

Did you love the way it slicked your skin like sweat
and made you glisten once the sun returned?
I remember that, Noah—the romance of the rain, its after-
glow.

But Noah, that's all over now, isn't it? I wonder
if you get flashbacks every time you see a cloud
a little gray of that awful day you tasted the apocalypse

and breathed its scent, first like petrichor and then like rot.
Oh Noah, you watched the rain fall and it didn't stop.
And now, no one understands your fear of rain.

And like you, I wonder how so many can love
spring and everything it brings—the wildflowers,
the birds returning and the earth's rebirth,

and the rainclouds and the storms, the thunderclap,
the floods, the awful feeling of the apocalypse
river down your throat or down your leg.

Noah, it's too much to live through it again,
another season of rain, of blooms, of so much loss.
Let's you and me go off into the desert

where the rain won't touch our skin. Where we can live
with dust and rocks and sand and barrenness,
hiding from the floods of grief within.

What If the Cranes Refused to Migrate?

What if one day the cranes refused to migrate,
decided that the continent should curve
to them and not the other way around?
They grew tired of rushing through the seasons,
of always living beak to beak, the landscape's
ability to feed them every year
diminishing like their numbers. They were weary
of dodging hunters' bullets down in Texas,
of searching for a place to build their nests
amongst the poisoned tar sands in Alberta.
They got sick of eating only waste
corn in the endless fields of Nebraska,
ever-sweeping up the farmers' messes.
They became fed up with always losing—
a mate, a chick, a sister, then a dule,
exhausted from migrations, moving, changing
with the world as climate changes, too,
then rushing to adapt, to make it work,
one more disaster coming at us now—
a flooded river, melted icecap, heatwave
beckoning them north a month too soon
and then, a snowstorm swoops in like an eagle.
What if a crane decides she will no longer
let the changes in the seasons ruffle
her feathers? What if all the cranes decided
this together, both the whoopers and the sandhills,
to stay put, give in to the impending
bird apocalypse? Why fly away?
Why not lounge for once, remain in bed
all Sunday afternoon instead of building
nests for a future that may never come?
Why tend the eggs to only have them crushed?

Why migrate just to starve or freeze or lose
yourself in spiraling towards Armageddon?
Oh God, our ecosystem would collapse.

I think of this one autumn afternoon,
in my bathrobe, staring out the window
as I watch a flock of sandhill cranes
beat their wings against the prairie wind.

How?

For Fannie Lou Hamer

As I learn the story of your life
in 2022, the year that choice
was ripped away, I wonder how you rose
the morning after your apocalypse—
when a doctor feared the awesome power
deep within your belly, so he took
it from you with a scalpel and a lie.

Fannie, how did you get out of bed,
missing a piece of you, that chance we get
at eternity, the ancient river
of your bloodline suddenly run dry?
How did you dress yourself or comb your hair,
or look into the mirror at the last
face that would wear your certain curve of beauty,
nourish the body robbed of something sacred?

How did you do it, Fannie? How did you
go on to brush your body off, to let that scar
on your belly heal, resist the picking of the wound
each day to feel its festering again
in your mind as it repeats the question:
why and why and why and why and why?

I'm asking, Fannie, as I'm staring up
at the ceiling fan that spins and spins
like the earth continues spinning on
as if this never happened, how to love
a world so fiercely that you want to save
it for other people's sons and daughters,
an unrighteous world that never will
hold your descendants in its tender arms?

Mollie's Canary, Spring

Your singing shatters the monotony
of wind. Your plumage brings a flash of gold
into this prairie winter's monochrome.
Sometimes, you even let me touch the softness

of your down and feel your racing heart.
Canary in the coalmine of my psyche,
warbling relentlessly to fill
the darkest crevices of memory,

the silence that was once a child's laughter,
you know that only I can hear your song.
No hen exists for miles and miles and miles.
But still, you feel the need within the hollow

of your bones, your throat, your sunny plumage
to call out to the phantom of your mate.
Do you gaze between cage's bars
and see infinity or simply snow

like me? As the canary-colored sun
comes up, perhaps awoken by your chipper
ditty, ditty, I can't help but hum along
and feel a tug of spring within my chest.

Prairie Dust

How to hold the whole of her within
your heart? You land here like a sandhill crane—

intending to move on as seasons change.
For now, the cottontails thump through grass.

Clusters of spiderworts blush indigo.
Some dawns, the sky can swallow you alive:

flesh and mind and soul. The wind keeps blowing
unobstructed, snarling your psyche.

A girl inhales the scent of corn and soil.
A farmer slaps his belly with a laugh

like the haunches of a sow that's off
to slaughter. You are here. You cradle this

moment in your arms as bits and pieces
of lullabies well up within your throat

and catch against your windpipe like a bone
as other words replace them on your lips:

silence, loneliness, Nebraska. They mix
with notes of laughter like a robin's song

that falls onto your shoulders, weighs you down
with a barrage of joy. Then you remember—

prairie's not a woman after all,
yet like your body, but a site of awful

beauty that's been plowed into submission.
Spring will come. It always does. The snowmelt

of this feeling washes everything
away like dust: the husks of last year's harvest,

the specks of memories, the pesticides.

The Beekeeper's Aubade

My love, I know that hives, like hearts, collapse.
This feeling comes most often in the fall
as I'm awoken by the morning's chill
and the horizon wears the hue of blood.

The workers keep the colony alive
with a grain of insect faith that soon
this prairie will explode again with clovers
like it used to years ago. But no,

the days of wild goldenrod have passed.
The workers visit dandelions, taste
neonics on their blooms. They feel the chew
of vampire mites that suck what little succor

the planet offers. One day, a worker bee
will just give up. She'll realize her wings
are too deformed, her viral load too high,
her spirit given out. She'll make a final

pearl of precious honey for her queen
cap the brood, and fly away without
so much as a goodbye, and then she'll die.
Her leaving is the sweetest kind of mercy—

the queen, her belly full, may yet survive,
slumbering in a sea of gold, her heart
oblivious and blissful as she makes
clutch after clutch of eggs in preparation

for the future that may never come.
I turn over in the bed and gaze
at your honeyed smile, your eyelashes
dusted still with sleep. But someone needs

to tend the bees this morning, so I rise,
dress in haste, and don my ivory veil.
I'll leave a pot of coffee for you, love,
and head into the frost to check the hives.

Pandora's Prairie

There's something in the endlessness that loosens
the psyche's lid: the butterflies traversing
these plains where every day's like every acre,
the sunlit grasses, high as hips, that sway

in unison, the cornfields hiding secrets
between their stalks. You imagine walking
through the rows, your fingertips caressing
silk—the first one brings a rush of pleasure

to the surface of your gooseflesh skin,
but the millionth one rubs it raw.
How many lifetimes would it take to swim
across this amber sea and reach the shore,

the mountains at the end of it that rip
a hole in heaven for your body's coming?
You know you'd never get there. You would drown
in the pandemonium of gold.

The jar, for now, sits fastened in your lap.
A kaleidoscope of question marks
flick their fragile wings against the lid
in preparation for the loosening.

If Babies Grew as Readily as Ears of Corn

A field of corn, Nebraska's open fields,
the body with its rows, the stalks erect
like gooseflesh as the last of winter's wind

blows through. What if these stalks could carry more,
first felt the fluttering of flesh within
their buds while basking in the summer sun?

In the stubble of September, you
walk into a field and stroke the silk
like a newborn's hair, the scent of earth

arising with the morning dew. You harvest:
bundle up the sheafs and tuck them in
a bassinet, your arms, your heart, both full

of golden joy at last. How rich you'd be,
and all the other farmers on the plains
with yields like this more valuable than gold.

You peel the husk and kiss the perfect ear.
You thank the Lord for every single one,
the first, the second, then a thousand more,

as plentiful as grain. The giving season
ends. The earth slips on her gown of frost
and settles in for months and months of sleep.

Brunch, 2021

This lazy summer afternoon, we brunch
at some bougie restaurant downtown,
something we haven't done for far too long.
We sit on the patio. I sip
a kale and apple tonic with some lemon
and lots of ice to quench that waking thirst
as the smell of fresh espresso wafts
out from the open door. The waitress hustles—
a full tray always in her hand, a smile
etched into her face. We ponder over
what to order, what to satisfy
a hunger that's been quarantined for months,
a year, a day, a lifetime now it seems—
hand-braided challah toast with maple syrup,
barbacoa tacos with tortillas
made from corn that's grown mere miles away,
steel-cut oats with marinated berries?
A cappuccino is a must, of course,
with frothy almond milk and local honey,
maybe a rose mimosa, too.
Wrapped in June's embrace, I could forget—
until the waitress interrupts, her smile
shattering as she sets my platter down:
organic avocado toast on multigrain,
topped with siracha and a cage-free egg
that bursts and drowns the plate in golden yolk.

Omaha in Winter

It's hard to be in love in Omaha
in winter when the downtown streets encase
in ice each morning as the city struggles
to get up, and snowplows move the mountains

of last night's storm. They gouge and scrape the pavement,
sullying the snow to match the sky,
the psyche. Trees case bony shadows west,
to the openness, the whitening

oblivion. The sun, exhausted now,
takes her time to rise before she starts
her crawl across the sky just to lie down
in the cozy bed of the horizon.

Most fly off and leave Nebraska when
she's in this winter mood, return in spring
when she dresses in forsythia.
But you remain to weather out the cold.

You hold what warmth is left against your chest
as frost begins to nibble on your earlobe
and the barren scent of winter's breath
settles on your hair, your skin, your heart.

Baby Dust

I'm sending all the baby dust your way,
She tells you with a smile like powdered sugar.

You wonder what it is, this baby dust
that everybody wants your body covered

with—a sprinkling of it to hide
this wound, this emptiness that no one knows

how to fill, not nature, faith, nor science.
But baby dust will do the trick. It must.

It's sweet and light and airy, cheap, no, free,
something she can toss without a thought

over her shoulder like a pinch of salt
that shoos away the devil from the kitchen.

You want to taste it, baby dust, the dulcet
flavor on your tongue that lasts a moment

then dissolves to nothing like spun sugar.
You know it isn't good for you. It's empty

calories. You know it isn't real,
nothing but a silly thing that people

say to be polite then change the subject.
And so, you shake it off, that baby dust,

and there you are again, a couple grains
cling to your skin like tantalizing hope.

Ode to My Mother's Stuffing

Confession time: I hate my mother's stuffing—
everything about it: how it soaks
up turkey guts for hours, how it's filled
with melted bits of celery and onion,
how many carbs and grams of fat it has
that I'd rather spend on pumpkin pie,
how she slips those secret raisins in
that never fail to make my stomach churn,
how it fills the mouth, sticks to the teeth,
slides down the throat, and sits inside the belly
for hours like a rock becoming guilt,
the aftertaste of which sits on the lips.

Thanksgiving stuffing is her pride and joy—
a recipe she's carried in her blood,
concoction that is womanhood, created
from the remnants tucked inside her cupboards.
Her mother made it, too, and stuffed herself
until her pancreas gave out. Her grandma
gobbled gobs of stuffing by the forkful,
learned a busy tongue can't speak the mind.

Each year, I swear will be the year I finally
tell mother how I hate her stuffing so.
But no. I grit my teeth. I grin. I bite
the soggy bread and raisins, and I try
to keep it down like an opinion,
because today's Thanksgiving after all,
and stuffing of the mouth is but tradition.

My Mother's Hair Is Falling Out

I comb my hair; a couple strands fall out.
Sunlight illuminates the flecks of gold.
This isn't something I should cry about—

like the rising oceans or the drought
halfway across the world. I try to hold
this grief within my belly. Hair falls out—

old strands must die so that the new can sprout.
I think about my mom, how she unfolds
her thinning ponytail. This is about

my ailing mother, seeing her without
her mane of femininity, rolled
and curled across her shoulders. Hair falls out.

Her hair has given way to scalp. No doubt
one day my golden hair will when I'm old.
This isn't something we should cry about—

her hair, my hair, and you—we're all en route
to that same place: the drain, the comb, the cold
earth. My mother's hair is falling out.
It's something I can't help but weep about.

How to Love a Maple Tree in Autumn

It's the perfect time to fall in love,
or so I tell myself. The days are shorter—
the sun is hustling across the sky
and night comes quickly to my doorstep.
It's the season where an apple tastes
like longing for the days we've left behind.
A cold front swoops in from the arctic,
turning cheeks the hue of sumac leaves.

The maple tree he planted at the edge
of the yard has slipped into its autumn robe.
The leaves begin to shimmer, twirl, and catch
the dying sunlight. How tenderly they drift
down to the lawn and look like dandelions
reminding me of that sweet season, gone.

I know what's yet to come, the haunting dance,
the gentle sinking into that long slumber
through the winter months. I'll watch that maple
lose its golden leaves like strands of hair
one at a time, until there's nothing left
of its beauty but its naked bark.

Soon, he'll rake the memories in heaps
of mulch and humus, haul them all away.
I wonder why I do this to myself
every vernal equinox—to fall
in love with what will leave me in its loess

Confession

She keeps a secret pint of ice cream stashed
inside her freezer, hides it underneath
a bag of peas and carrots, last year's mashed
potatoes, chicken breasts. Some nights, her sweet teeth
bring her to kitchen—hungry, naked.
The freezer opens and it glows, the moon
shining on her skin like something sacred.
Ready to devour, she wields a spoon.

Here's the confession: she is every woman,
swallowing the sugar and the spice
she hoards in herself when no one's looking—
deep within the psyche's pit, where ice
ensures the sweetest things will never age.
This ice cream is a metaphor for rage.

Pandora in Omaha

Some nights, I see Pandora in my dreams.
She opens up my body like a box
and out flies everything I am. I wake,

wondering if it's another nightmare
or a reverie of what's to come.
In the milky dawns, I see her sometimes

at the park, especially in spring
planting pansies in flowerbeds,
her body stooped, her bare hands in the earth,

or sitting on the bench, an empty bottle
at her side. She asks for change, for me
to unzip my purse, but I refuse.

While driving down the highway, I imagine
her in the fields of corn, between the rows,
opening the ears to glimpse the gold.

I hear her voice beneath the prairie wind,
Don't you want to know what's trapped inside
your husks? And yes, I do, but no I don't.

III.

BROKEN INTO
BLOSSOM

Flo and I Hike along the Platte

I'm trying to enjoy the burr oak's golds,
       the maple's reds, but God, these cramps are Hell—

ruining this afternoon just like
       so many pairs of panties, bedsheets, nights

that could have broken into blossom if
       it wasn't always autumn in my life.

I want to hike without abandon, see
       the pirouetting of vermillion

foliage splashing into flowing streams
       that whisk them deeper through the scarlet woods

where deer tracks slip into the gully's mud.
       I want to watch these torrents flush this forest

of its memories, its fallen leaves,
       witness how a season of debris

empties at the mouth into the Platte.
       I want to feel the magic of this body,

how it makes room within the womb
       to bloom again come March, the blossoms

now nothing but a feeling underneath
       the surface of this forest's sodden skin.

I know the sanguine leaves give birth to spring,
       but my lady parts are hurting like a bitch.

Paloma Wings

I wondered why maxi pads have wings,
and what the use of wings are
if all they do is hold you in place.

As a kid, I imagined a flock of them,
of maxi pads,
taking to the sky like startled palomas,

outstretching their white wings
and using them to get as far from me
as possible at that time of the month.

I thought that wings
were only used to fly away—
to touch the sky like Icarus,

who never had to wear a maxi pad.
Who would ever want to be grounded
in such a place, the delta of a river,

to collect the flotsam left behind
from the wreck of another month?
Because when you're thirteen,

you learn there's nothing worse
than yourself, a girl,
the red red red of you.

The Deposit

Is not the goal in life to leave the world
better than you found it? Hovering
over a merlot stain on the carpet,
I wonder if, for me, it's possible.

A rag in hand, I splash some vinegar
on the scarlet stain that marks my past—
the evenings spent here in this living room,
carelessly creating disarray,
covering up messes with a rug
on the beige savannah of this carpet.

The kitchen's passed the point of no return—
how many oil spills have slicked the ocean
of its wooden floors, how soot has gathered
in the crevices from burnt mistakes,
and how the scent of garbage lingers still.

The bathtub flooded once. The seas are rising.
The smoke alarm went off. Rainforests burned
a continent away. As climate changes,
the air conditioner blasts through the summer.

Why did I let my microcosm go?
In this age of the Anthropocene,
where apartments tower high like forests,
each one a planet edging towards destruction.
And now, I'm trying to erase the trace
of my mistakes, turn in my keys, and migrate
to a new apartment I'll rent from the earth,
a swathe of land that I'll let go to Hell.

I think of all of this while vacuuming
one final time, removing, hopefully,
the last of my dead skin, my hair, my body's dust
from this place, and pray against the odds,
the mighty landlord refunds my deposit.

Her Golden Goose

Such a gosling is a fragile thing:
emerging from a golden egg, blood-streaked
and alabaster, tail feathers slicked
with sheen, its budding beak a point of pleasure.

Flecked with shell, it still belonged to her
and her alone, a quiet fluttering
within her skin, a sunrise in her darkness,
a breath of burning air that smelled of summer.

It was hers, then it belonged to someone
else once downy fluff turned into feathers
and feathers into sky. It had a name
she only whispered to herself—the softness

but a memory of adolescence.
Some nights, her fingers touch that velvet still,
the part of her that once could make her bedroom
shadows dance before it flew away.

She calls it back. Most seasons, though,
her golden goose is continents away.
But sometimes, it can hear her midnight calls,
comes home to roost with her nest of flesh.

Tangles

Every day I wake to this: a pit
of tangled hair, a labyrinth, an ember,
and a shelter all at once, a rhumba
of rattlesnakes in slumber with their eyes
peeled, gazing like a pair of die.

I grab the brush. It hisses, knows its worth—
this feral mop top made of wilderness.

Some days it wants to frame my face in strength,
a lion's mane, a symbol that this woman's
got better things to do than tame her hair.

Some days it wants to hang down like a rope,
tied in a ponytail and dangling
for invited paramours to climb.

It remembers history—the battles
it always won of split ends, tugs, and curses
flung from mother's spit to daughter's snarls
for centuries, the painful yank of bullies
on the raucous playgrounds of our lives,
being chopped off, faded, bobbed, and pixied.

These tresses know what lies between the strands,
what hides atop the nape, and like Delilah,
the power of a pair of snipping shears.

But it also knows it always grows again—
a meadow overrun with dandelions
every spring, or it can be a nest
for sparrows, mockingbirds, or even falcons.

Some have said that tangled hair is sin,
serpent, and temptation. Nothing scares
this head of tangled hair. There's something deep
within these roots, the follicle, the psyche
that keeps it wild, growing, and persisting,
this daedal wonder made of mystery,

this crown I wear each night when I untie
the bun and let it fall, a flood of pleasure,
strength, and joy that rushes down my spine.

My Mother Explains How to
Grow an Avocado from a Pit

It isn't hard. Just slice into the flesh.
Any old, sharpened knife will do the trick.
The pit grows in the belly of the fruit—
you have to scoop it out. A spoon is best
so you won't nick its skin. Then get a toothpick;
pierce it through the seed. This step is vital,
though it's always hard for me to do.
Nothing grows without a little pain.
Then fill a glass with water, let it soak
up the sun and hope against all hope
you didn't screw it up this time. Then wait.
That's hard as well. I check it every morning,
hoping to see a little hint of green.
Once it sprouts, it's time to tuck it in
a pot and dote on it with water, patience,
sunlight. The hardest part is yet to come:
realizing that the seedling's grown
too big to stay inside the kitchen, knowing
it needs a place to spread its roots out far
away from your watchful eye. You have to wait
a lifetime, though, to see your labor's fruits.
It's worth it, but you'd better plant it soon.
How quickly avocado flesh turns brown.
How fast this ripening. You blink and then
it's too late to enjoy. But if your seedling
takes root and grows, you know there's more to come.
How abundantly the body gives—
how miraculous, a root, a leaf,
a heart. How we, like everything, go on.
daughter, see, it really isn't hard.

While Quarantined, I Make a Pot of Beans

Today, I hunger for some normalcy,
so I pull my stockpot from the cupboard.
It wears the years upon its surface, scratches
and dents from countless moves, the tumbles
it took, the ashy aftermath of flame.
The pintos chatter as I pour them in.
I inspect them for the errant pebble
amongst the speckles. Then, I fill the pot
with water from the tap and let them soak
in the refrigerator overnight.
This task requires boundless patience,
a commodity in short supply
like toilet paper, bleach, and baby wipes.

When morning comes (just like it always does),
I drain the pot of yesterday and fill
it up again with water, then I wait
for it to start to boil on the stove.
Pinches of oregano and garlic
go into the pot. The scents of earth,
memories, and comfort rise with bubbles,
fill the kitchen with a warm embrace.
As I chop cilantro, I taste spring
blooming deep within my roiling belly
as it blooms outside, oblivious
of the virus or our quarantines.
As I slice the onion into slivers,
I think of how we all come from the earth,
and how, no matter what, we will return.
As I dice a jalapeño pepper,
I think of how we all have seeds of power
tucked within the membranes of ourselves.

I dump them in the steaming soup of succor.
They simmer for a couple hours more
before I add a rubescent tomato.

Our mothers and our grandmothers all knew
a pot of beans could fill the emptiness
of countless bowls, of bellies, and of hearts.
So, they cooked them in their tidy kitchens
as their worlds, too, were threatening to end.

Why I Never Mow My Lawn

As far as all the neighbors are concerned,
there's nothing worse than lovegrass taking over
the yard, or blades of witchgrass flourishing,
showing her bare seeds to the cul-de-sac.
Oh dear, the chickweeds with their alabaster
petals are about to bloom. The foxtails
curl and flop. A patch of clovers whiten.
Stinkgrass spreads without a lick of shame.
Sunflowers open up their golden petals,
like a robe, for all the street to see
the ochre button that invites the bees
to come and touch the center of themselves.
Each spring, I love the saturnalia
of weeds, the scattering of smutgrass, sandburs
gently prickling my tender skin,
the morning glories pink and filled with glory.

The HOA has other plans and issues
a citation: *Mow it down or else!*
I'll take the ticket, Thank you very much,
and wade into my sea of towering grasses,
to feel their tickle on my naked legs.

Ode to the Flint Hills

How I long to be like you, Flint Hills,
sea of grasses taller than a man,
bluestem and switchgrass rippling in endless
auburn waves that froth with alabaster.
The vast expanse of you remains unchanged
for eons and for acres, beautiful,
immaculate, and wild. You symbolize
the grace of nothingness, in letting go
of yourself, of bathing in the golden
streams of sun, in grasses growing wild,
in spreading out and taking up your space.

I idolize the endlessness of you—
how when your sisters one by one all fell
to the farmers' plows and you refused,
too difficult, too rocky, and too tough
to be anything but wilderness.
You know that you could never be a cornfield.
You refuse to nourish anything
but whom you choose to cradle in your flesh,
from booming prairie hens to hungry bobcats,
groves of cat-claw briar to red-tailed hawks,
and in the towers of your grasses, bison
and their gleaming, helpless calves each spring.

How every year you burn yourself to ashes.
How every year you rise anew again.
How every year you find the strength to flourish.
Flint Hills of Kansas, bastion of tallgrass—
you were too challenging to civilize.
You're everything I wish that I could be.

Mollie's Canary, Autumn

This morning, the canary wouldn't sing.
The quarry of his heart filled up with poison
from the prairie wind and me. Last spring,
his singing harmonized with all the voices
of the thrushes and robins. Now
silence overcomes the house. Outside,
he sees warbler on a maple bough.
I watch him as he watches it, decide,
in a moment's madness to unlatch
his cage's door and let him fly away
into the bleeding morning. May he catch
joy before becoming winter's prey.
Still, I envy how he chose to fly,
and for a season, got to taste the sky.

As Wildflowers

I think I've found a cure for all the shame
we were taught to feel within our bodies:
instead of flesh and bone, imagine this—
a wildflower blooming on the prairie.

As a black-eyed Susan, it makes sense
to wear a yellow sundress, gussy up,
and gaze into the mirror of the sky.
Being lovely isn't frivolous:
it's an ecosystem of survival.

No one dares to blame the spiderworts,
who fill the summer fields with indigo,
for seeking out the touch honeybees,
for flirting with the monarchs flying by,
for relishing the kiss of August sun.
And who could blame the hoary vervain blooms,
who drip with dulcet nectar, for enjoying
a visit from a handsome hummingbird?

And if my body were a dandelion,
I wouldn't have to hate it so for changing
as the seasons change—its golden petals
suddenly the hue of winter's snow.

Mollie's Pansies

This is how I mark the land as mine:
a tiny flowerbox, a bed of straw,
the mornings I spend kneeling at this shrine
to blossoming against the odds, the awe
within my chest when, finally, it blooms
thanks to my tenacity. This year
it's scarlet like a blushing cheek, the plumes
of rufous hummingbirds who flutter here

for a moment's dalliance of sweetness,
the bloodshot sunset. Meanwhile, on the plains,
wild violets flourish, fill the bleakness
lavishly with their amaranthine stains.
But I must have *my* flowers, don't you see?
This pansy clinging on to life is me.

Elizabeth Ann, the Black-Footed Ferret

Once, they were as plentiful as sin,
but then, we knelt before the gods of grain
and expelled her mother to the badlands
where all of them would dwindle off and die

to extinction's brink. Such is the story
of keeping faith alive like animals
in captivity: we tend to it,
force-feed it nutrients, and inbreed it

as it paces in the cage within
and languishes until there's nothing wild
left in the heart. But scientists believe
she's coming back, a single female ferret

at the Frozen Zoo, preserved for decades.
A clone, she rolls extinction's stone aside
and resurrects a different breed of faith.
May she be the savior of her species.

Tumbleweeds

This land was once a prairie,
empty of everything

but ecosystem. Now:
a clean swept street, a row

of garbage cans, our beige
houses popping up

like dandelions in spring,
the green St. Augustine

of every lawn with sprinklers,
fertilizer, mowers,

white picket fences, not
a single weed. And then,

they came in roving hordes
bunching in the streets

one windy afternoon,
blocking the driveways, climbing

high so they could reach
the rooftops. Millions

of them, brown and dying,
desperate mothers searching

for a place to dig
their roots into the soil.

As they tumbled through
suburbia, they scattered

seeds on this precious lawn,
taking back their Eden.

Afraid of the Dark

When you're little, you're afraid of darkness—
the layer of it underneath your bed
that hangs like heavy fog beneath your body,
always waiting for a glimpse of you,
the dangle of your nightgown's edge, your naked
ankle, or your bunny slipper's nose,
so it can dig its claws into your flesh
and pull you deep into its frothing gloom.
You fear its pointed canines made of shadows.

But now, you're older and you know that darkness
isn't tangible, but still can pull you underneath
its waves, can wake you in the night with fear
as it fills your nostrils, makes its way
deep into the ringlets of your brain,
make the heart feel heavy with it, bones
stiff with it. So, when it fills your psyche
like a patch of haze that washes over
the meadow of mood, you still don't dare
to leave your bed in fear of what might seep
from underneath it, what might pull you down
deeper into this. What is it, darkness?
That feeling in the crevice of yourself?
And how to trust in morning's swift arrival?

You know this, snug inside your somber bed:
A shadow's tooth can't pierce your calloused skin.
A gust of wind, of change, can banish fog.
Darkness melts like butter in the sun.

Starting Anew

This McMansion is too new to harbor
ghosts—no creaking floorboards, attics empty
for generations, secret basement rooms
where one might hide. You left those heavy shadows
and those sins back East with all the bones
you pick, too cumbersome to haul along.

These plains are inhospitable to shadows—
no crevices in which to hide, no hills
to stop a somber silhouette from stretching
to oblivion. It's all laid bare
across this empty landscape. In this house,
there is no clutter—ancient work boots caked
in the mud of yesterday, moth-chewed
quilts that wear the odor of the past,
teacups stained with rings of russet coffee
and the lipstick of your grandmother,
long dead and turned to loess. Your ancestors
had no room within their covered wagons
for delusions. On the new frontier
danger was tangible—it had a face
of heavy clouds, the scent of rain, the voice
of howling wind and whistle, and the touch
of a fist against the fragile jawbone.

Now, in this new house that smells of fresh
paint and the dust of sheet rock, her descendent,
You—from generations forward, sweep
the floor of all the prairie dust you track
on the porcelain tile and wipe the windows
by moonlight with ammonia to find
not phantoms, but your own hard-scrabbled face,
gazing deep into your weary eyes.

Abell 2744

Tonight, the city lights of Omaha
all but drown the stars in milky haze.
It looks like nothingness surrounds the moon,
though, of course, I know this isn't true.

I wonder where Pandora's Cluster is,
that distant burst of pink and lavender
with its halo made of afterglow,
leftover from rupturing of worlds—

too far away to glimpse, and yet somehow
I feel it underneath my flesh, the site
of its collision, where celestial bodies
met like skin to skin, like palm to cheek,

the clash of bones. It's comforting to know
that even stars can't hold themselves together
in the face of loss and make disaster
something beautiful to fill the darkness.

Maybe, after all the rocks, debris,
and vapors slip out from that box of space,
a tiny thing called hope remains inside.
Here on earth, my sky's forever changed.

Headlights

I find it hard to tell my father this,
so at the dinner table I explain
the headlights on my car are going dim.

It's an easy metaphor: the headlights
are my hope, the night is my despair.
He knows this, too. He takes a sip of beer.

This darkness is a monster we can't name,
not as a father and a daughter, no.
It's something we can't talk about—

the body and its failures and his longing
for a child when I was but a dream,
that monster of a longing in me now.

But this, a dimming headlight, yes, it's something
he can fix, something his hands can do
to quell the shadows of the road ahead.

We finish dinner, then he gets to work.
My father takes my keys. My father pops
the hood. My father takes away what's dying

and replaces it with light. If only
it was easy to restore the bulbs
within this broken flesh, within the soul.

If only I could switch hope on again,
alighting the front yard as evening washes
over the cul-de-sac that is my heart.

Be safe, he says, before I pull away
into the sable night, and for this moment
the street ahead of me is bathed in gold.

Ode to the Sickle Moon

I love the sickle moon, a sickly thing
hanging in the dark, a rib bone jutting
into the sable flesh of sky. This moon
is easily forgotten, overshadowed
by memories of moons that scintillate
the skyscrapers, that make the street dogs howl,
or illume the eyes of prowling cats.
But this skinny moon, this waning moon,
gleams with the same light on her ashen skin.
And though she's barren, pocked with yesterday,
a crater for a belly, she resolves
every cycle to come back from darkness,
the brink of it, to pull herself out, somehow,
someway, and given time, returns to fullness.

Hymn for the Gray Wolf

Gray wolf, now that you are coming back,
rolling extinction's mammoth stone aside
with a nimble nudge of your wet nose,
and returning to your keystone throne
in these woods, I ask for your forgiveness.

We've sinned for centuries. We hunted you,
blamed you, and wore your power like a coat.
We mistook your feral majesty
over these forests for a reign of terror.
We crucified you, banished you away,
and called you demon just because we feared
your piercing gaze that saw straight to the evil
in our bones. You smelled it on our skin.
From you, we couldn't hide it anymore,
and so, we sent you to oblivion.

But you are the epitome of grace—
you embody it with ashen fur,
canines, and those haunting hazel eyes.
We begged for your return, and then you came,
resurrected from the brink of death
by the miracle of nature's power.
You forgive, forget, and thrive again
with equal parts ferocity and mercy.

With moonlight scintillating from your mane,
you howl your redemption hymn for us.
May it fill the forests of our hearts.

Self Portrait as a Ghost Town

A century ago, I felt alive—
the bustle of a busy afternoon
in the town square, lovers calling out
to one another from their balconies,
gardens tended with the utmost care.

Sometimes I miss those busy days. Today,
I am a crossroads for the tumbleweeds.

The crumbled ruins of an ancient schoolhouse
that once held children in its arms of bricks
lay silent, burdened only by the sky.

The roofs gave in, collapsing one by one.
The shattered glass of windows form mosaics,
creating bursts of luster in the rubble.

The empty oil wells creak as wind blows through.

As the years go by, I've let it go
to Hell—the ryegrass and the wild oats
reclaim this swathe of dust like scabs that cover
a gaping wound that never healed quite right.

Come sit with me and learn to see the beauty
in this brokenness. A blazing sun
sets upon these hollowed bones of buildings
returning to the earth with dignity,
brimming with humus, ash, and honeysuckle.

Her Apocalypse

I think this is how our world will end:
a mother, finished with the giving season,
feels the coming warming of her body.

Rivers of sweat begin to swell and drown
what used to be nesting place of us.
Icecaps sag into the rising seas.
Hurricanes of grief and joy make landfall,
rocking the body's shores. A trembling
beneath the surface changes everything—

Red knots refuse to don their breeding plumage,
kaleidoscopes of golden monarchs thin
leaving bald spots in the ecosystem,
the blooms of wild sage each March no longer
overflow like blood across the prairie.
They fade to but a trickle, then they cease.

This is how it ends, no glorious
fanfare but a quiet revelation
in her bones that this is it—the season's done.
Our mother gazes at the stars and wonders
what new beginnings menopause will bring.

Tomato Season

A dying plant, more brown than green, continues
its slow march towards giving up on spring
and everything it brings. I rescue it
from the dumpster's dark abyss, and wonder
what kind of person could have thrown in there
in a moment of despair or carelessness.

Other tomato plants are green and blooming,
some branches sagging with the weight of fruit.
When everything is swelling like the moon,
but you're in wane, it's hard to keep from blaming
yourself, your roots, and not the fallow soil.

So, I water it each morning, trim
its shriveled branches, offer it support.
But living things don't just snap back from trauma
even as the morning showers us
in streams of gold. All through tomato season,

I have to learn to love it just to love it,
not for its fecundity, the promise
of months of sweetness, seeds, and rosy flesh,
but for the scrawny plant it is today,
clinging to life but empty, still, of fruit.
I understand. Why give the world your harvest
when it's filled with so much withering?

As November seals tomato season
shut, I bring my plant inside and set
it in the slants of winter sun that thrust
through the dusty windows of our place.

I notice this: a single yellow flower
clawing its way into existence, petals
reaching towards the ashen sky above—
on its own time and against all odds.
My wilted psyche blossoms, too, with hope.

The Windfarm

Walnut, Iowa

Another windstorm blows through Iowa
as dust and darkness fill sky. There's nothing
you can do to stop what's coming next—
disheveled hair, the billowed dress, a tousled

psyche. You can't stop the oak from losing
another limb to the calamity,
the stalks of corn from lying down and never
rising from their earthen bed again,

the newborn foal from tumbling to the ground.
As the shingles on your roof let go,
the shushing of the wind is all you hear,
and in the lull of it, his heavy sigh

at the windswept sight of you. You know
what happens if you let it carry you
into the oblivion of all
it's taken from your arms: the child's balloon

you watch fade into sky. Outside your window,
windmills wave their moonlit blades hello.
You hear their moans but never see them stop.
This is how to deal with such blusters:

harnessing their power. So, you stagger
through the darkness of your bedroom, flip
the switch, and suddenly, you're bathed
in golden light that almost feels like dawn.

ACKNOWLEDGMENTS

I am grateful to the editors of the following publications where some of these poems have appeared previously:

"At Lewis and Clark Landing," *Tipton Poetry Review*

"Summer of Lightning Bugs," *Texas Poetry Assignment*

"Sunday Mornings," *Better Than Starbucks*

"Recipe for Fudge," *Texas Poetry Assignment*

"Manifest Destiny," *One* (Jacar Press)

"For My Brother," *Writing Texas*

"Eve Quarantined," *Wonderous Real*

"The News" *San Antonio Review*

"Prairie Dust," *San Antonio Review*

"Beekeeper's Aubade," *Summerset Review*

"Pandora's Prairie," *Literary Imagination* (Oxford UP)

"If Babies Grew as Easily as Corn," *The Pierian*

"Brunch, 2021," *Texas Poetry Assignment*

"Omaha in Winter," *Tipton Poetry Review*

"My Mother's Hair Is Falling Out," *West Trestle Review*

"Confession," *Rathalla Review*

"Pandora in Omaha," *The Pierian*

"Paloma Wings," *Stained Anthology*

"Flo and I Hike Along the Platte," *Juked*

"The Deposit," *I70 Review*

"While Quarantined, I Make a Pot of Beans," *Texas Poetry Assignment*

"Why I Never Mow My Lawn," *Indianapolis Review*

"Tumbleweeds," *Border Crossing*

"Self-Portrait as a Ghost Town," *Switchgrasss Review*

In addition, some of the poems in this manuscript were previously published in my chapbook, *Prairie Madness* (North Dakota State University Press, 2021). The chapbook was awarded the Poems of the Plains and Prairies Prize and was a finalist for the Eric Hoffer Book Award.

* * *

Thank you to the fantastic editorial staff of Cornerstone Press for making this book what it is today. I am immensely grateful to Karlie Harpold and Paige Biever for their careful, astute editorial eyes. Thank you, Allison Lange, for your creative vision for this book. Thank you to also to Samantha Bjork and Sophie McPherson for helping to shepherd these little poems out into the world. And thank you, Dr. Ross Tangedal, for creating such an amazing experience for both your students and your authors. Cornerstone Press truly is something special, and I am so honored to have worked with this dynamic, talented, and passionate team of publishers.

KATHERINE HOERTH is an associate professor of English at Lamar University in Beaumont, Texas, and a member of the Texas Institute of Letters. She is the author of several poetry collections, including *Flare Stacks in Full Bloom* (2022), *The Lost Chronicles of Slue Foot Sue* (2018), *Goddess Wears Cowboy Boots* (2014), and *The Garden Uprooted* (2012). She is the 2015 recipient of the Helen C. Smith Prize for the best book of poetry in Texas and the 2021 Poetry of the Plains Prize from North Dakota State University Press. Her 2021 letterpress chapbook, *Prairie Madness*, won honorable mention for the Eric Hoffer Award. Her work has been published in numerous literary magazines including *Summerset Review, Valparaiso Review,* and *Southwestern American Literature.*